稀世珍宝

大 熊 猫

Rare Treasure — Giant Panda

世にも稀な珍寶——パンダ

张德重 摄影

四 川 美 术 出 版 社

瞩望大熊猫

马安信

如帆，远方的海枕着一千年的眺望；如雷，远天的闪电劈开一万年的呼唤！打开凝聚着摄影家汩汩心血的画集，我走进了许多关于大熊猫的充满传奇的记载，走进了唐代诗人白居易题于屏风之上的《貘屏赞》，走进了莽莽青藏高原东部边缘的高山深谷。在浓密的竹海里，花团簇拥的草地上，接近白云的地方，我看见了它们——大熊猫。

我所热爱的这一稀世物种，它们是一个神秘的家族，拥有一个神秘的世界；我所热爱的这一稀世珍宝，它们憨态十足，正在时光的流水中洗浴、漫步。或姊妹相依相偎，似在诉说悄悄话；或花丛悠闲漫步，俨然一幅盛世图；或四脚朝天、抱头而卧，极尽风趣与幽默；或做出许多让人捧腹开怀的动作，铺展出悠闲自得的形象与意趣；或时而低问嫩竹，时而仰问天空，并用潮湿的鼻息将云层推远……

阳光就这样笔直地洒下来，在它们毛绒绒的脊背上像瀑布一样倾泻；蓝天就这样无垠地铺开去，在它们笑容可掬的脸庞白云一样流淌。它们留下的足印深深浅浅，但都标出了爱的走向；它们是吉祥和安宁的象征，也是和平与友谊的使者。

一棵草死了，人们忽视它。不像一个人，死亡是那么直接、突然，让人触目惊心。那么，与我们人类共享一个生存环境的大熊猫呢？读着摄影家这本大熊猫的画集，我读出了一句闪亮的箴言："谁在等待中希望谁就丧失希望！"是的，摄影家手中的相机一如旷野的风，在人类的大地上深深刻下了一行粗犷的大字：瞩望大熊猫，关爱大熊猫，拯救大熊猫！

2003年5月8日于蜀都诗梦书斋

Gazing at Giant Pandas

Ma Anxin

The distant sea is resting head on a millennial overlook, just like the sail; remote lightning in the sky has cleft a myriad call, just like the thunder! On opening the picture collection full of crystallization of the camerist's painstaking efforts, I read plenty of legendary records of giant pandas, enjoyed *In Praise of Tapir Screen* written on the folding screen by Bai Juyi (a poet in the Tang Dynasty), and came close to high mountains and deep valleys at the east edge of the vast Qinghai-Tibet Plateau. In the thick bamboo sea, on the lawn dotted with magnificent flowers, near the white clouds, we saw them - giant pandas.

The rare species I love is a mysterious family who owns a mysterious world; the rare treasure I love is charmingly naive, bathing and strolling in the passage of time. Some of giant pandas like sisters lean close to each other as if they were whispering in private; some wander leisurely in the flowers in clusters, just like a picture of peace and prosperity; some lie down and clasp their heads with four feet towards the sky, how humourous they are; some take a lot of actions which split our sides with laughter, showing their easy and self-congratulated images and interests; some eat tender bamboos or look up at the sky with moist snuffle. Their moist breath will push cloud layer far···

So the sunlight scatters straightforwards, pouring like a waterfall on their fluffy back; the blue sky rolls out so boundlessly that the white clouds are flowing along their smiling face. No matter how deep and shallow their footprints are, they mark the tendency of love; they are the symbol of fortune and tranquility, envoys of peace and friendship as well.

If a blade of grass dies, people may neglect it. But for a person, his death is so immediate and abrupt that he would be stocking by the sight. Then, how about the giant pandas sharing the same subsistent environment with us human being? When reading the camerist's picture collection about giant pandas, I have found a brilliant admonition: "He who lays his hope in waiting will lose hope!" Yes, the camera in the camerist's hands, just like the wind in the field, has engraved a line of unpolished characters deeply on anthropic ground: Gazing at giant pandas, showing solicitude for and taking good care of them and saving them!

on May 8, 2003
Shudu Poem-Dream Study

パンダに目を注ごう

馬安信

　帆のように，遠方の海が千年の眺めに枕しており，雷のように　空の果で稲妻が光って萬年の呼び掛けを切り開いた！撮影師の心血を凝らしたこのアルバムを捲って見ていると，パンダについての，傳奇にみちた記戴に引きつけられて，恰かも唐の詩人白居易が《貘屏贊》と題した屏風繪に入ったか，青海チベット高原の東端の高山深谷に入ったかのような氣分になった。深く茂っている竹の海で，花むらにかこまれた芝生の上で，白雲に近い所で，この目で見たよ，カレたち──パンダを！

　私の熱愛する世にも稀なこの生物種類，これは，神秘な家族で，不思議な天地を持っており，私の熱愛する世にも稀なこの珍寶，カレたちは，溢れるようにおぼっこくて，月日の流れを浴びて，足の向くままに歩いたり，花むらの中をゆったりと散策したりして，まるで盛世のような繪を展示してくれる。仰向きに寝ころんだものもいれば，頭を抱えて横たわったものもおり，實に趣とユーモアの極みを盡してくれる。腹をかかえて大笑いをさせるような多彩な動作を見せたり，顔を下に向けて柔らかい竹に聞くか，空を仰いで何かを聞きたがるかのようにしたり，その濕った鼻息で雲層を遠くへ押そうかとしたりしており…

　日光がたきのように，まっすぐに，そのふかふかと柔らかい背中に降り注いでいる。青空が果てしなくひろがっていて，カレたちの，白雲のような笑顔にすれすれに流れている。殘したその踏み跡が凸凹になっているが，愛の行方を示したものである。カレたちは，吉祥と安寧のシンボルであり，平和と友誼の使者でもある。

　一本の草が枯れはんだのは，往往にして人目に無視されてしまうが，人間にとっては，死亡はそんなに直接的で，突然のことで，心を痛ましめるものである。そう言えば，私たち人間と共に一つの生存環境を樂しんでいるパンダにとっては？このパンダアルバムを見ていて，私は，光っている一言の箴言をよみ取った："希望を待つことにする人は，きっとその希望を失ってしまうのだ！"　そうだ。撮影師が手にしているカメラは，野原を吹き撫でた風のようで，人類の大地に力強く次のような言葉を刻んでおいた：パンダに目を注ごう，パンダを大切にしよう，パンダを救おう！

2003 年 5 月 8 日
蜀都詩夢書齋にて

大家好！我是大熊猫。
Hi, Everybody! I'm a Giant Panda.
皆さん，こんにちは。わたしは　大パンダです。

兄弟姐妹在一起，比什么都快乐
Happiest When Living Together with Brothers and Sisters
兄弟そろって起居をするのは，何よりです。

哺乳
Breast-feeding
赤ちゃんに母乳を飲ませているところ

乐园
The Paradise
わたしたちのパラダイス

嗨，竹子真好吃啊!
Hey, How Delicious the Bamboo Is!
はあ，竹は　じつに美味しい!

我们的生活多美好！　What a Nice Life We Have!　わたしたちの生活，なんと樂しいだろう！

我们的生活多美好！　What a Nice Life We Have!　わたしたちの生活，なんと樂しいだろう！

春色満园
Spring Scenery All over the Garden
春色まさにたけなわ

爬树能手
Experts in Climbing the Trees
木登りのベテラン

熊猫故乡——卧龙

Pandas' Homeland —Wolong

パンダの古里——卧龍

妈妈你别走
Don't Go Away, Mum
ママ，はなれていかないで

姐妹
Sisters
おねえさんといもうとさん

豆蔻年华
A Budding Beauty
青春を楽しむ年ごろ

幽梦又还乡

Dreaming of Returning to His Native Place

夢の中でまた古里に帰った

牙好胃口就好
Good Appetite with Good Teeth
はもいいので，美味しく食べられる

玩竹
Playing with Bamboo
竹遊びをしているところ

从远古走来
Coming from the Remote Antiquity
遠い昔から来たんだよ

呐喊
Shouting Loudly
聲をあげて吼えている

站　Standing　立っている

登　Climbing Up　登っている

望　Gazing into the Distance　望んでいる

两对双胞胎
Two Couples of Twin Pandas
二ついの雙子

天之娇子
Pride of Nature
生まれつきの人氣者

29

高瞻远瞩
Taking a Broad and Long View
高みに登り遠くを眺めている

妈妈到国外去了
Mum Having Gone Abroad
ママが外國へ行ってしまった！

遐想
Indulging in Reveries
遥かに思いを馳せている

交流
Exchange of Views
打ち明け話をしている

2 1

4 3

34

攀缘四步曲
Four Steps for Climbing
よじ登りの四步曲

温馨之家
Warm Home
心温まる家庭

鲜花盛开的时节
Time in Full Flowers
花の盛り頃

闻声起舞
Dancing at the Sound
歌聲を聞くと，すぐダンスを

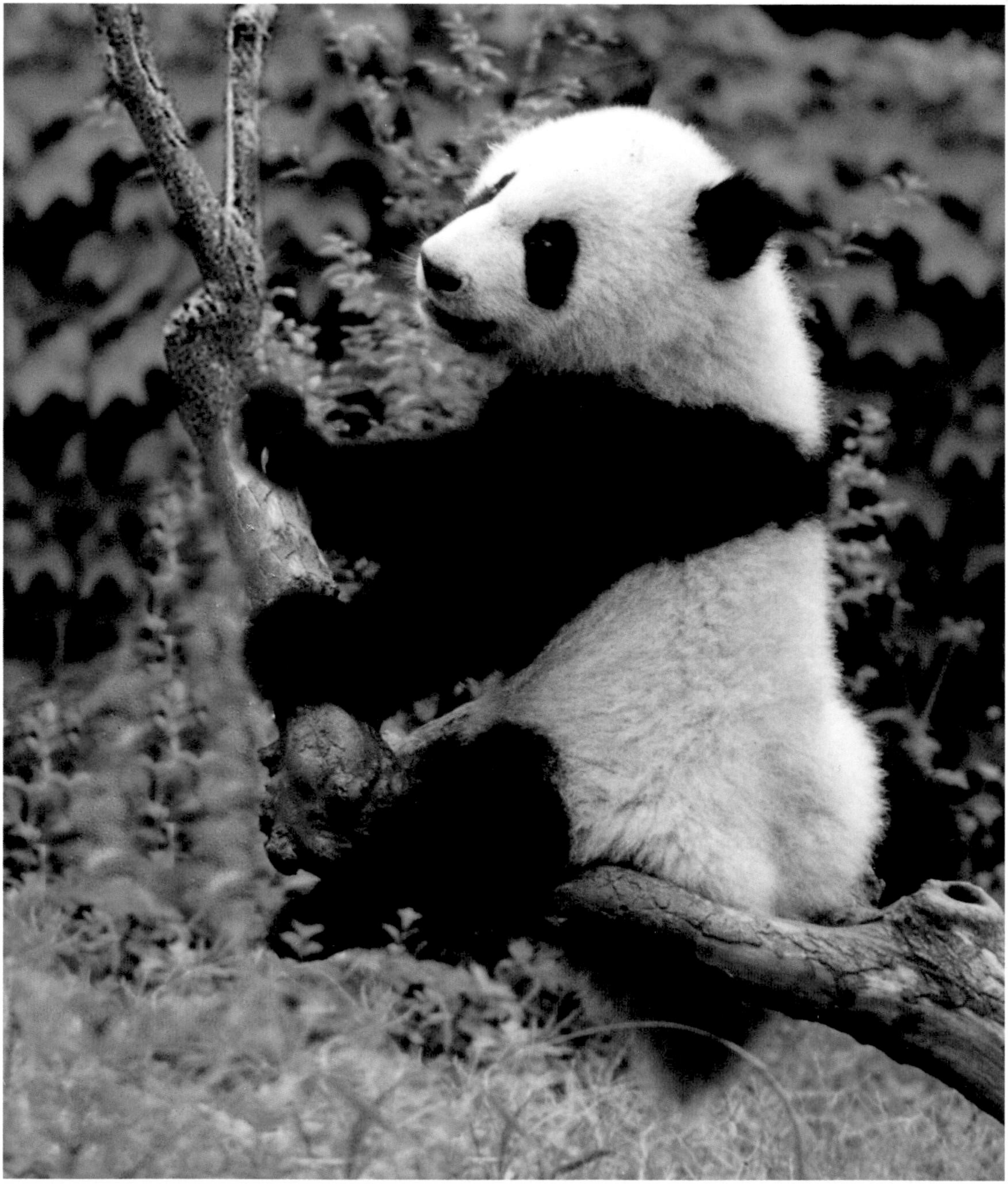

潇洒骑士

A Natural and Unrestrained Knight

スマートなナイト

风流飘逸
Distinguished and Elegant
のんきな姿

树杈小憩
Taking a Rest on the Crotch for a Little While
木のまたで一休みしよう

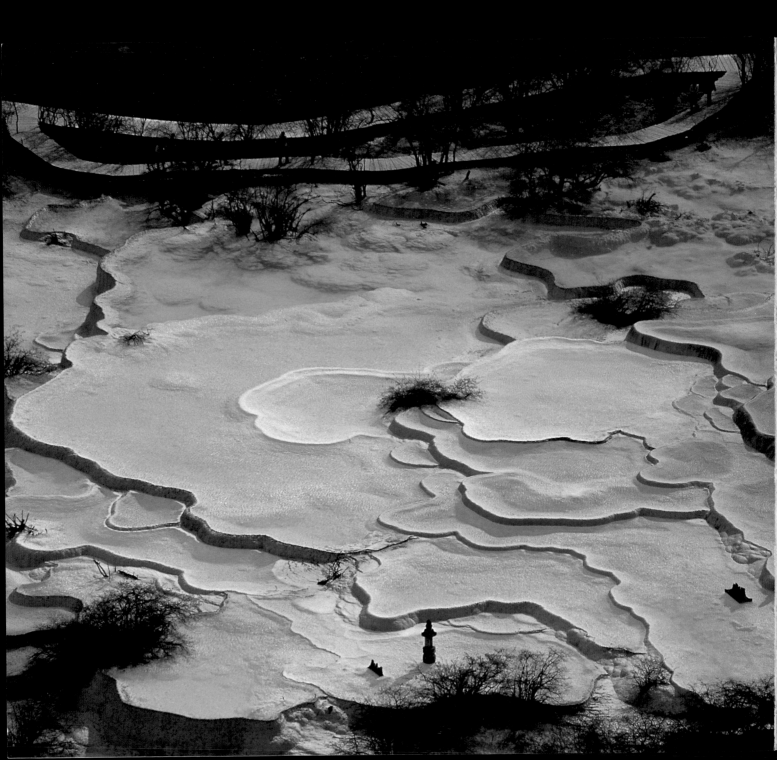

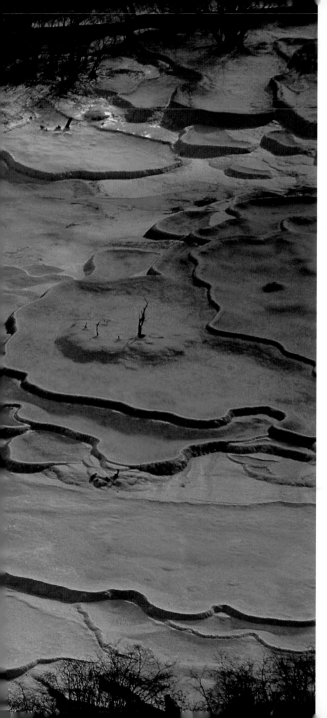

熊猫故乡 —— 黄龙
Pandas' Homeland —Huanglong
パンダの古里——黄龍

倚浓荫，任清风吹拂
Let the Breeze Brush Past Against the Shade
木かげで涼風當りに任せよう

虎视
Eyeing Covetously
虎のような目付き

演出开始了
The Performance Is Beginning
演出が始まった！

丰盛的午餐
Sumptuous Lunch
ゆたかなランチ

春情绸缪
Sentimentally Attached to Spring
思春の年でろ

幸福的一对
A Happy Couple of Pandas
幸せないっつい

宝宝出生了：出生3天、10天、22天、36天的幼仔
Baby Pandas Come into the World: The 3-Day, 10-Day,
22-Day and 36-Day Young Pandas after Birth
ベビーが生れた：生れて3日　生れて10日　生れて22日
生れて36日

母子情依依
Mother Panda and Her Children Affectionately Sitting Together
なごりおしい親子

65

你争
Contending with Each Other
きみ, 取っていこうか

我夺
Competing with Each Other
ぼく，うばいとるよ

各吃各
Each Eating Its Own Food
食べ物は，おのおのの分を

妈妈教吃竹
Mother Panda is Teaching Her Child How to Eat Bamboos
ママが教えたとおりに食べている

蓦然回首

Hastily Turning Its Head

不意に振り返ったシーン

真好玩!
How Funny!
ああ，楽しいね。

荡秋千
Playing on a Swing
ぶらんこのり

悬挂
Hanging
吊り姿

仰望
Looking Up
見上げ

吃饱了
It Is Full
もうお中いっぱい

喝醉了
It Is Drunk
よっぱらった！

尽情享用
Enjoy Eating as Much as Possible
好きなだけ享受しよう

给我吃一口
Let Me Have a Mouthful of Food
ぼくにも一口食べさせてくれ

哇，我要倒了!
Oh, I'm going to fall!
わあ，ぼく，倒れそうかな！

蹬技
Juggling with the Feet
枝を踏み付けて登っている

手脚并用
Climbing with Hands and Feet
手足を同時に使っている

各自东西
Lying Feet to Feet
それぞれ東西にいる

摔跤　　Wrestling　　レスリング

出浴
After Taking a Bath
—風呂浴びた

涼爽极了!
How Cool It Is!
なんと涼しいだろう

87

向上挤　Hustling Up　上のほうへ押して

偷　枝
Stealing a Branch
こっそりと　枝を取った

向下滑　Sliding Downwards　下のほうへ滑ろう

林中玩耍
Playing in the Woods
林の中で遊んでいる

有人类的关爱，我们不会从地球上消失。We won't disappear from the earth with the love of mankind.

人類の關心にあずかって，わたしたちは地球から消えることナシ

国宝的风姿
Charm of the National Treasure Pandas
國寶の風采

国宝之神韵
Verve of the National Treasure Pandas
國寶のすぐれたおもき

熊猫故乡 — 宝兴蜂桶寨
Pandas' Homeland —Fengtong Stockaded Village of Baoxing
パンダの古里——寶興蜂桶寨

憧憬未来
Yearning for the Future
未来に憧れている

图书在版编目（CIP）数据

稀世珍宝——大熊猫／张德重摄. —成都：四川美术出版社，2003.5

ISBN 7-5410-2208-X

Ⅰ. 稀... 　Ⅱ.张... 　Ⅲ. 大熊猫—中国—现代—摄影集 　Ⅳ. J429.5

中国版本图书馆CIP数据核字（2003）第031014号

稀世珍宝——大熊猫

责任编辑：林　桃

翻　　译：连　益（英文）
　　　　　陶法义（日文）

封面设计：华　熔

责任校对：倪　焱

四川美术出版社出版发行

（成都盐道街3号 邮编：610012）

新华书店经销

四川省印刷制版中心印刷

开本：880mm×1192mm 1/24 印张：4.5

2003年6月第一版 2003年6月第一次印刷

印数：1-5000册

书号：ISBN7-5410-2208-X／J·1958

定价：50元